Bits and Pieces

Start collecting bits and pieces to make the wonderful pictures in this book. You'll need paper and card, wool and felt, sequins and beads, foil, glitter and paints, sponge and fancy sweet wrappers.

You can either make the pictures just the same as the ones in the book, or you can use the ideas to design your own. There are all sorts of exciting and unusual painting techniques for you to try out as well.

Acknowledgements

Designed by **Jane Warring**
Illustrations by **Lindy Norton**
Pictures made by **Karen Radford**
Photographs by **Peter Millard**
Created by **Thumbprint Books**

First published in 1994 by
Hamlyn Children's Books
an imprint of Reed Children's Books,
Michelin House, 81 Fulham Road, London SW3 6RB
and Auckland, Melbourne, Sydney and Toronto

ISBN 0600 58288 4

Printed and bound in Belgium by Proost

Making Pictures
SECRETS OF THE SEA

Penny King and Clare Roundhill

Contents

HAMLYN

A Sandy Sandcastle

Decorate a sandpaper castle with fancy paper shapes, pebbles and seaweed, and put a bright flag on the top. To make the seaweed glisten, dip strips of green tissue into PVA glue. Why not try to decorate the beach too?

Bits and Pieces
- Stiff blue paper
- Paints & brush
- Stiff card
- Scissors & glue
- Sandpaper
- Pebbles & shells
- Green tissue
- Sweet wrappers
- Coloured paper
- Sponge
- Cocktail stick
- Straws

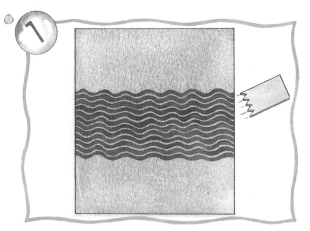

Brush blue paint over the middle of the stiff blue paper. Make wiggly waves (see paint tip).

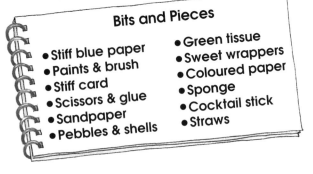

Cut a beach and a sandcastle out of sandpaper. Glue them on to the background paper.

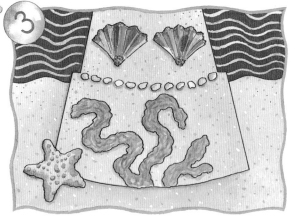

Decorate the castle with sweet wrappers cut into fans, tissue seaweed and tiny pebbles.

Decorate the picture with shells, a bucket, a sponge sun and starfish. Don't forget a flag!

PAINT TIP

Cut a small rectangle from stiff card. Snip triangles along one edge to make a painting comb. Cover the paper with thick paint. Drag the comb through it to make swirly shapes.

7

Lurking Lobster

Let your hands and fingers create the sea creatures in this underwater picture.

You'll need to practise a bit to get perfect lobster, crab and shrimp prints.

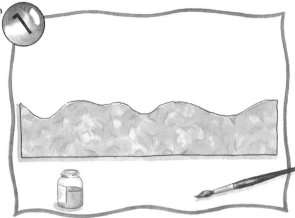

Cut a sea bed from white paper. Brush yellow paint over it. Crumple it. Smooth it out.

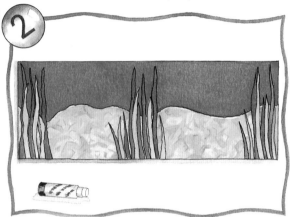

Stick it on to the bottom of the stiff blue paper. Glue on strips of green tissue seaweed.

8

Bits and Pieces

- Sheets of white paper
- Scissors
- Paints & brush
- Stiff blue paper or card
- Glue
- Tissue paper in different shades of green
- Black sequins or beads

Make lobster, crab and shrimp prints on white paper (see paint tip). Cut them out.

Glue the sea creatures on to the sea and sand. Stick on black sequins for their eyes.

PAINT TIP

Cover the side of your little finger with paint. Press it on to white paper to make shrimps. Do the same to print the legs and claws for the lobster and crab. Use the palm of your hand to print the crab's body and the side of your hand for the lobster's body. Make thumb prints for the lobster's tail.

9

Terrific Turtle

Use any colours you want to make this shiny turtle. Draw around the yoghurt pot on to the background paper to see where to position his head, legs and tail. Tape the fish on to bendy pipe-cleaners and stick them all over the sea.

Bits and Pieces

- Empty plastic yogurt or cottage cheese pot
- Thick shiny paper
- Scissors & glue
- Stiff green paper
- Glitter
- Shiny card
- Red sequins
- Tissue paper
- Pipe-cleaners
- Sticky tape

Cut the shiny paper into little squares. Glue them in rows to the sides and base of the pot.

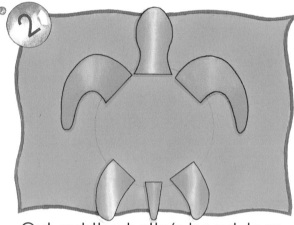

Cut out the turtle's head, legs and tail from shiny card. Glue them on to stiff green paper.

Glue the pot in position for the turtle's body. Decorate it with glitter. Add red sequin eyes.

Make paper fish with tissue fins and tails. Tape them on to pipe-cleaners and then to the sea.

PAINT TIP
Instead of using shiny paper,
you can paint the fishes'
bodies. Draw them on plain
paper and paint them bright
colours with pretty patterns.
Cut them out and add tissue
fins and tails.

Jolly Jellyfish

Make these jolly jellyfish floating in the deep, dark sea. Use shiny silver foil for their bodies and lots of glittery, coloured pipe-cleaners for their tentacles.

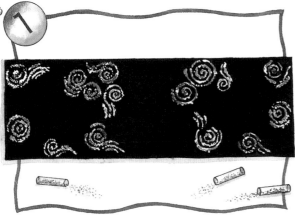

Cut a long piece of stiff black paper. Dab swirls of glue over it and cover them with glitter.

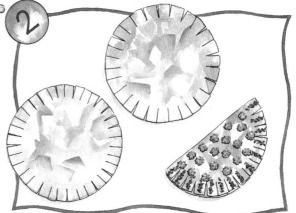

Draw and cut out circles of foil. Snip the edges. Fold them in half. Add glitter.

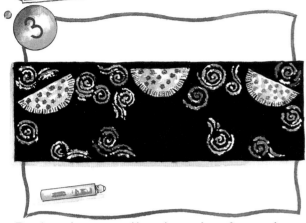

Bits and Pieces

- Stiff black paper or card
- Glue
- Glitter in lots of different colours
- Silver foil
- Pencil
- Scissors
- Glittery pipe-cleaners
- Sticky tape

PAINT TIP
Instead of using black card, paint your own background. Brush thick black paint over white paper. Let it dry. Paint on another coat.

Dab glue on the back of each folded circle. Stick them on the background paper.

Tape glittery pipe-cleaners on the inside of each jellyfish, like this. Fold them in half again.

13

A Fabulous Mermaid

Make a picture of a pretty mermaid from card or felt. Give her woollen tresses, a sparkly tail and a smiling face. Make her jewels out of shiny paper and tiny beads. Then put her in the deep, swirly sea with lots of colourful seahorses.

Bits and Pieces

- Light blue card
- Blue paint
- Sponge
- Pink card or felt
- Pencil
- Scissors & glue
- Wool & ribbon
- Gold glitter
- Ric-rac
- Shiny paper
- Beads & sequins
- Couscous

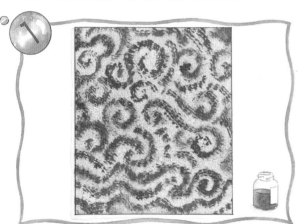

Sponge the dark blue sea on top of the light blue card (see paint tip). Let the paint dry.

Draw a mermaid on pink card or felt and cut her out. Glue her in the middle of the sea.

Decorate the mermaid with a glitter and ric-rac tail, wool hair, a bow and shiny jewels.

Stick cut-out card seahorses on the sea. Glue on a couscous and gold glitter sea bed.

PAINT TIP

Put dark blue paint in an old saucer. Dip a small sponge into the paint. Dab it in swirls over the light blue background card to give the effect of big frothy waves.

Paddling Toes

This silly picture of feet paddling in the sea will make people laugh.

Use dried beans for the pebbles and tissue paper for the feet and legs.

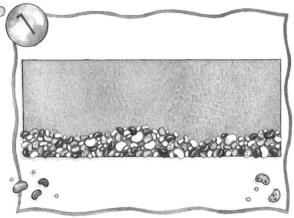

Cover the bottom of the stiff blue paper with strong glue. Stick on all sorts of dried beans.

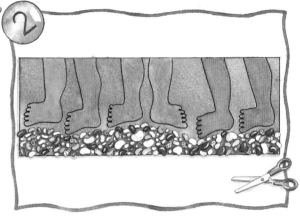

Cut three pairs of tissue legs and feet. Stick them down so they are standing on the beans.

PAINT TIP
Cut a fish shape out of a sponge. Pour some paint into a saucer. Dip the sponge fish in the paint and print it on to the picture. It is best to practise first on a sheet of paper before you print on to your picture. You may need to use slightly thicker paint or make it a little more watery.

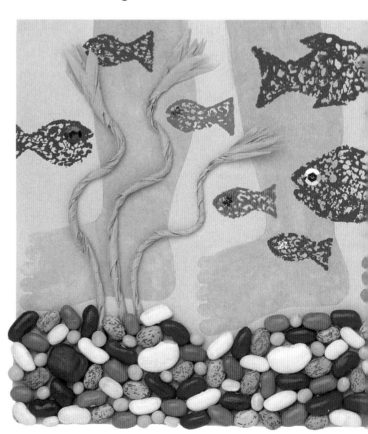

Bits and Pieces

- Stiff blue paper
- Mixed dried beans
- Strong glue
- Coloured tissue paper
- Pencil
- Scissors
- Bits of sponge
- Paint
- Old saucer
- Newspaper

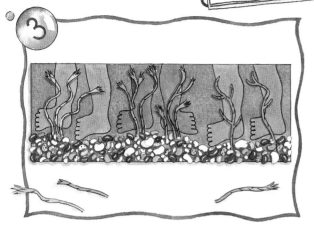

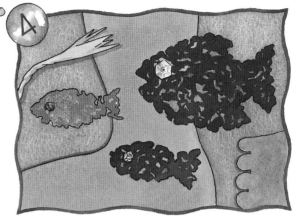

Cut little strips of green tissue and twist them into seaweed. Glue them on to the sea bed.

Make a sponge fish (see paint tip). Print fish in lots of different colours over the sea and legs.

17

Under water world

Use an old shoebox or a cardboard box to make this underwater garden. Fill it with colourful fish, a seahorse, lots of pretty shells and some wiggly seaweed. You can also add a chest overflowing with sparkling treasure.

Bits and Pieces

- Shoebox
- Paints & brush
- Shiny green paper
- Scissors & glue
- Shells
- Small pebbles or sand
- Stiff card
- Sequins or beads
- Needle & thread
- Sticky tape

Paint the box blue (see paint tip). Cut out paper seaweed fronds. Glue them to the box.

Spread the bottom of the box with glue. Stick small pebbles or sand and shells all over it.

Cut fishy shapes out of card. Paint them with spots or stripes. Glue on sequin or bead eyes.

Thread cotton through each fish. Knot it. Hang the fish with tape from the top of the box.

PAINT TIP

To paint a box really well,
it is best to paint the inside
first. Let it dry, then turn
the box over and paint the
back and sides. Use thick
paint and a big brush to
cover it with lots of layers.

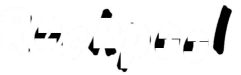

A Rippling Rockpool

Cut a rockpool shape from blue paper. Cut a smaller white one the same shape.

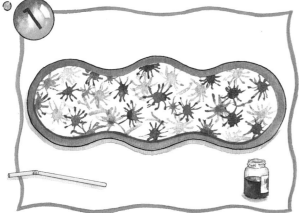

Blow blobs of paint over the white paper (see paint tip). Glue it on to the blue paper.

Fill the pool with leafy fish and ripples, surrounded by a fringe of crêpe seaweed.

Cut four strips of blue and green crêpe paper. Snip a fringe along each one, like this.

PAINT TIP

Before you start, cover your work surface with newspaper as this is a bit messy. Put drops of watery blue paint on to white paper. Gently blow the drops through a straw to make the paint spread in all directions. Instead of using only one colour, you could try blowing several different colours, one on top of the other.

Bits and Pieces

- Stiff blue paper
- White paper
- Scissors
- Glue
- Blue paint
- A straw
- Pale and dark blue and green crêpe paper
- Sticky tape
- Leaves
- Tiny beads

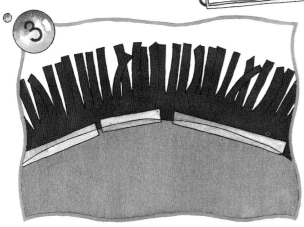

Tape the crêpe strips, one on top of the other, to the back of the blue paper. Fluff them out.

Cut big and small fish shapes out of leaves. Stick them on to the rockpool. Add beady eyes.

21

A Grasping Octopus

Look at how much treasure this lucky octopus has in his eight long arms! Paint one of your own, floating in a blue sea. Give him treasure galore, made with shiny bits and pieces you can find around the house. Put a gold crown on his head.

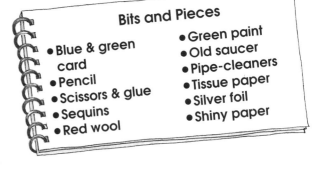

Bits and Pieces
- Blue & green card
- Pencil
- Scissors & glue
- Sequins
- Red wool
- Green paint
- Old saucer
- Pipe-cleaners
- Tissue paper
- Silver foil
- Shiny paper

Draw an octopus on green card. Glue on beady eyes and a red wool mouth. Cut him out.

Fingerpaint dark green suckers on the arms (see paint tip). Stick the octopus on the blue card.

Twist two pipe-cleaners into a ring, make a necklace of tissue balls and a foil goblet.

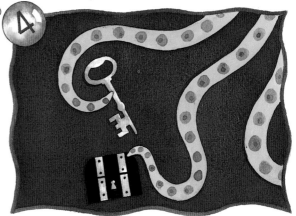

Cut other precious things from shiny paper. Glue one on the end of each tentacle.

PAINT TIP
Put thick paint into a saucer.
Dip in your little finger. Make
sure it is well coated. Print
paint blobs on the paper
with your fingertip.

23

Fish in a Net

Save lots of colourful sweet wrappers and shiny paper to make flashy fish for a picture like this. Put some of the fish in a net with bobbing cork floats and string. Cover the bottom of the sea with seaweed and lurking sea creatures.

Bits and Pieces
- White card
- White candle
- Paints & brush
- Shiny paper
- Pencil
- Scissors & glue
- Sequins
- Fine fruit net
- String
- Cork circles
- Coloured paper
- Tissue paper

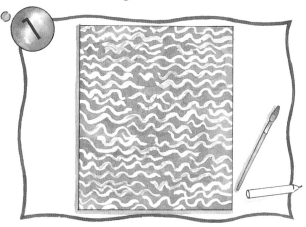

Make waxy waves all over the white card and cover them with blue paint (see paint tip).

Draw fish on shiny paper. Cut them out. Decorate them with paper shapes and sequin eyes.

Stick fish in the net and on the sea. Thread string through the net. Glue cork circles on top.

Cut out tissue seaweed and paper sea creatures. Glue them on to the bottom of the sea.

24

PAINT TIP
Draw wavy lines all over the
piece of paper with the
thick end of a candle. Brush
watery blue paint over the
paper. The wax lines will
show through the paint.

25

Whale of a Time

Have fun blowing bubbles to make a frothy sea for these whales to swim in.

Cut out a frilly border of green seaweed to frame your underwater picture.

Mix some blue paint, a squirt of washing-up liquid and a little water in a large bowl.

Put a straw into the mixture. Blow hard until bubbles puff up above the rim of the bowl.

PAINT TIP
To make clean bubble prints, lay the paper gently on top of the bubbles. Be careful not to press the paper down on to the rim of the bowl. After each print, blow the mixture again to make more bubbles. If your paint mixture is not bubbly enough, add a little more washing-up liquid.

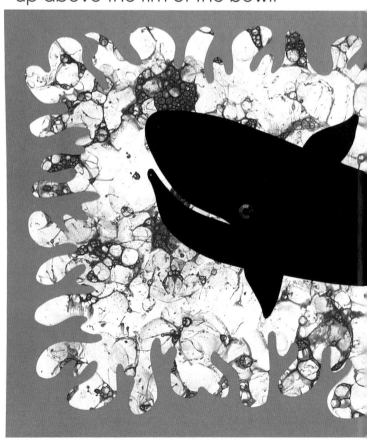

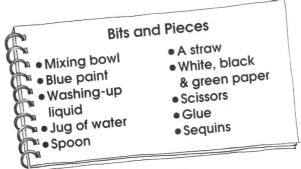

Bits and Pieces

- Mixing bowl
- Blue paint
- Washing-up liquid
- Jug of water
- Spoon
- A straw
- White, black & green paper
- Scissors
- Glue
- Sequins

To make a foamy sea, cover a long sheet of white paper with bubble prints (see paint tip).

Stick two black paper whales on the sea. Glue on sequin eyes and a green paper border.

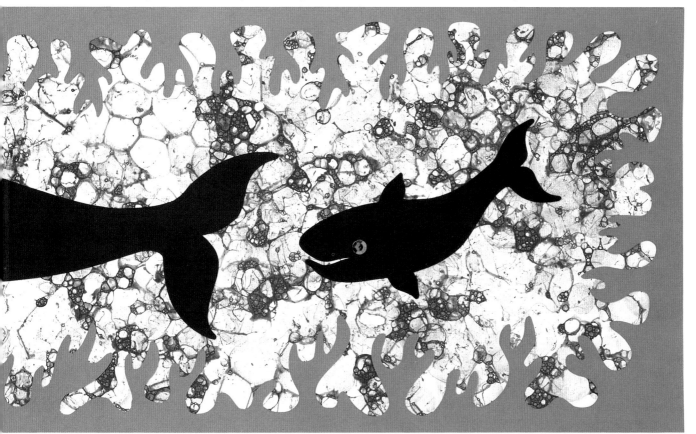

Sparkling starfish

Create an unusual picture of colourful felt starfish washed up on a beach made of lentils, beans and barley. To make the starfish sparkle and glisten, cover them with pearly beads and sequins. Print a fishy border with potato-cuts.

Bits and Pieces

- Yellow and green card
- PVA glue
- Dried lentils, beans & barley
- Scissors
- Felt in different bright colours
- Beads & sequins
- Big potato
- Saucer & knife
- Paints & brush

Spread glue over the yellow card. Cover it with lentils, beans and barley, like this.

Cut out two big and two little starfish shapes from different brightly coloured felt.

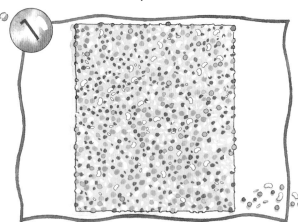

Stick the starfish on the lentils. Press down hard. Decorate them with beads and sequins.

Stick the lentil-covered card on the green card. Make a potato print border (see paint tip).

PAINT TIP
Cut a big potato in half.
Ask an adult to help you cut
a fishy shape out of each
half. Put paint in a saucer
and press the potato
cut-outs into it. Print
them on to green card.

29